Costume Reference 5

The Regency

MARION SICHEL

Publishers   PLAYS, INC.   Boston

First published 1978
© Text and illustrations 1978, Marion Sichel

First American edition published by PLAYS, INC. 1978

Library of Congress Cataloging in Publication Data

Sichel, Marion.
    Costume Reference.
       Includes bibliographies and indexes.
CONTENTS: v. 1 Roman Britain and the Middle Ages — v. 2 Tudors and
Elizabethans — v. 3 Jacobean, Stuart and Restoration — v. 4 The
Eighteenth Century — v. 5 The Regency
1. Costume — Great Britain — History
I. Title
GT 730.S48 1978   391 .00941
76-54466   0-8238-0217-5   (vol. 5)

Printed in Great Britain

Contents

The fashionable riding habit with the sloping shoulders and full long skirts. Lady on the left has a braided close-fitting jacket. Lady on the right has lace-edged shoulder capes. Both have top hats with long flowing veils, c. 1835

Introduction

This, the fifth volume in the *Costume Reference* series covers a much wider span than the Regency period. We start at 1800, when George III (1790-1820) still reigned (although increasingly troubled by bouts of madness). He was forced to hand the crown to his son, the Prince Regent, in 1811 and the Regency proper lasted until 1820 when the old king died and the Prince Regent took on the full title of King George IV. After George IV's death in 1830, William IV reigned until his death ushered in the Victorian age in 1837.

Apart from this succession of kings, regent and a queen in a comparatively short space of time, there were other factors making for rapid change. In England the Industrial Revolution and reforms in agriculture which had started earlier in the eighteenth century were now making a great impact on life, and costume, of course, reflected this. Britain was, by this time, the leading industrial nation with a prosperous middle class. It was this class which, more and more, made its influence felt in matters of taste. On the whole the dress of the period tends to be more sedate, conservative and less exuberant than the extravagance of some eighteenth-century styles with their hoops, massive wigs and striking cosmetics.

The French Revolution of 1789 had triggered off immense changes throughout the whole of Europe and by 1800 Europe was locked in war — a war which lasted until the battle of Waterloo in 1815. Perhaps it was because England was cut off from its traditional source of fashion inspiration — Paris — for so long that it developed a style of men's tailoring which was to dominate the European fashion scene.

The lady on the left is in a three quarter length pelisse or carriage dress trimmed with fur and is wearing a casquet or helmet type bonnet. c. 1812. The lady on the right is in a light, full to the ground, high waisted Empire style dress c. 1821. The gentleman is in a Brummel fashion with the cut away coat and the 'M' shaped notched high standing lapels. The trousers were fastened under the shoe c. 1811

The man who has traditionally been seen as the genius behind this new 'English' style is the remarkable George Bryan Brummel (1778-1840), better known as 'Beau' Brummel. Although he is the most famous dandy of all time, he was not interested in the frivolous, but rather strove after a perfection of cut which expressed his ideas of 'good taste'. Thus, he took the riding and hunting costumes of the day and, with the finest, plain cloths available, made them as well-fitting as possible. Often the various garments were made by different craftsmen, experts in their particular field. The secret, if indeed it was a secret, was the unobtrusiveness of the style, gone were the bright colours and superfluous embellishments — the key-note was simplicity.

This simplicity can be seen also in women's costume. The early years of the century saw the culmination of a fascination (started in the eighteenth century) with ancient Greek, Roman and Egyptian cultures. In France this classicism expressed itself in high-waisted, flimsy dresses known as 'Empire line'. They take their name from Napoleon's declaration of himself as Emperor of France and her Dominions in 1804. It was a fashion which, amongst a few, pushed itself to the limits, with completely exposed breasts, in a desire to imitate the supposed custom among the ancients.

With Beau Brummel's fall from favour in 1816 and the Restoration of the Bourbon monarchy in France in 1815, simplicity gave way to a frenetic experimentation with different modes — extravagant stays, enormous leg-on-mutton sleeves supported by wire frames — a period of quick-changing fashion which was soon to be cooled by the new influences of the Victorian era with which we shall deal in the next volume.

Men

Suits were comprised of coat, waistcoat and trousers. When worn informally the coat was similar to a dressing gown and called a *morning gown* or *banjan* which were ground length, loose and tied at the waist. They had no back vents and were worn mainly in the mornings with a cap and slippers. They were very fashionable, made in expensive silks and brocades. They were also known as 'deshabille', from the French word meaning undress.

COAT

A *skirted coat* was worn throughout the first half of the nineteenth century. The coat skirts were so cut as to form coat tails at the back. These were divided by a vent into two, the tops were pleated and ended with a hip button. Pockets were inserted in the pleats or else a pocket with a flap was placed each side of the skirt at the waist. Flaps were normally rectangular, but could be scalloped as previously, this being mainly the fashion for Court wear.

The skirts at the front of the coat ended at waist level and were sometimes cut horizontally to meet the back tails — a style reminiscent of the present-day 'dress coat'. Another style had the front curving down from the last button to the back as the contemporary morning coats of today.

The *collar* was of the stiff stand-fall type and if the coat had lapels, the notch between the lapel and collar could be M or V shaped. The M-form was where the collar met the lapel, this notched shape eased the turnover of the collar and was popular until about 1855, and indeed continued

The lady is in a day dress with the fullness down from the shoulders and caught at the wrist. These are known as imbecile sleeves. The fichu pelerine is caught and tied at the wrist. The gentleman is wearing a frock coat style with a velvet waistcoat. c. 1834/5

into the 1870s for evening wear. The lapels could have buttons on the turned over parts.

The narrow coat *sleeves* were wrist length and ended in either a cuff or a side slit closed with two or three buttons.

There were several styles of coats. A *double-breasted* type with the fronts overlapping and a double row of buttons, one row for fastening. The front skirts were either square cut or rounded with the tails at the back square. The sleeves were long and plain, and the collar had lapels. Another style named after the Frenchman who introduced it, known as *Jean de Bry,* had a high stand-fall collar and the sleeves were gathered and padded at the shoulders to give a 'kick-up' effect. From about 1820 most double-breasted coats had a separate piece of material for the buttons and buttonholes. This was known as a 'button-stand', and was very practical when the garment was worn closed, as it took the strain from the main material of the coat.

The *single-breasted* coat had two to three buttons down the front which sloped away from the waist with rounded tails.

If worn for morning wear coat *buttons* were mostly plated. For the evenings the coats were mainly dark blue with flat, gilt buttons.

The body of the coat had only three seams, one either side and one at the centre back, the side seams being set more towards the rear. For evening wear the coat was so tight that it was almost impossible to button up, thus the waistcoat, shirt and cravat were revealed. About 1818 the body of the coat became longer and better fitted at the waist, so that the crease formed by this tightening was removed by inserting a dart or 'fish', which by the 1820s became a seam. This meant that the coat body had five seams, with the introduction of a separate piece of material under the armholes to the waist.

The *collar* during the 1820s and 1830s was large and stiff, being lined with buckram and the front of the coat was padded. The collar with a plain or M notch at the turn of the lapels could often have buttonholes. Pockets could be waist high with flaps or be concealed in the pleats.

The *sleeves* which were gathered at the shoulders and reached the wrists ended with side slits and two or three buttons and a stitched down real or sham cuff. This style of sleeve was called a 'French riding sleeve', the cuff being known as a 'French cuff'.

The gentleman on the left is in a morning suit with a tailcoat and the trousers strapped under the foot. The gentleman on the right is in a short redingote which is trimmed with braid frogging known as Brandenburg. c. 1838

The *frock coat* appeared about 1816 and could possibly be traced to a military type coat worn at the Battle of Waterloo in 1815. It was at first single-breasted, buttoning from the neck down to the waist or just below. The collar was either the rolled or stand-fall variety called a 'Prussian' collar. The fitted body at first had a dart and then a seam at the waist. The full skirts hung straight down and the back had a vent with side seams and buttons on the hips, the length of the coat varying in the earlier years. The Wellington frock, popular about 1818, had a horizontal fish at the waist which later developed into a waist seam. In the 1820s the waist lengthened. The sleeves had a 'kick-up' at the shoulders and had slit or plain cuffs. To keep the military image, the coats were often decorated with braids and frogging.

By the 1830s and 1840s the frock coat was the most popular for informal wear. It became shorter and ended at about the thighs, padding still being used over the chest. The high collar and wide lapels sometimes reached the shoulders. There were hip pockets under flaps or in the pleats, and sometimes also a breast pocket on the outside.

There were several other styles of frock coat. The Petersham frock coat which was double-breasted, had a double row of four buttons, a broad velvet collar, and lapels and cuffs to match. The Taglioni frock coat was single-breasted with a narrow collar and lapels with skirts fairly short and full.

The *surtout*, which could also be worn as an overcoat was either single- or double-breasted with a velvet collar, outside breast pocket, and was usually worn closed.

In the 1820s the morning coat or tail coat was usually double-breasted, whereas the evening coat was mainly single-breasted. The collar was high at the back, the falling part only coming down partially, to join the low rolled lapels with a V or M notch. The double-breasted coat lapels were large, whilst those of the single-breasted types were smaller.

The cut of the body of the coat to the tails was usually square at waist level, with the coat tails short and wide. Buttons often decorated the pleats of the skirts and at the waist the flapped pockets were not very large. Sleeves were gathered at the shoulders and padded and were known as 'en gigot' (leg-o-mutton) from about 1824. The chest and shoulders were also padded. (After about 1832 gathering at the shoulders became less popular, although a little remained until the late 1840s.)

Single-breasted tail-coat with full at the shoulder sleeves tapering to the wrist. Close-fitting single-breasted waist-coat. Tight-fitting pantaloons of a jersey material were held by a strap under the instep, c. 1825

Fashionably dressed man in a double-breasted tail coat, deep M-shaped collar. Short-waisted waistcoat and close fitting knee breeches c. 1807

Double-breasted coat with the full skirts cut away in front and a wide shawl-type collar. Wide 'sailor' trousers of nankeen were worn, c. 1836

The *morning* or *riding coat* was a tail coat with sloping front edges instead of a straight cut, and was worn mainly, as the names indicate, for riding, which was a popular morning pastime. The coat was mainly single-breasted with a large collar with lapels in the 1830s. From about 1838 it was called a 'Newmarket'. The back vent had hip buttons and pleats. Flapped pockets and an outside breast pocket were sometimes used. For riding the coat was usually dark green, whilst for hunting the favourite colour was red.

WAISTCOATS

Waistcoats were usually to waist length, single- or double-breasted, with or without collar and revers. Until about 1825 they were usually square cut whereas after that date they could be slightly pointed at the centre front. A standing collar was popular until about 1830.

In the early 1800s they were usually single-breasted and square cut just visible beneath the front part of the coat body at waist level. Of the five to six buttons, the upper ones were left open to reveal the frilled shirt.

Fronts were padded slightly and a dart under the lapel and armhole helped create the fashionable fullness to the chest in the 1830s and 40s. Waistcoats were one of the most fashionable and decorative parts of a man's attire and were made in rich and embroidered materials. Sometimes even two waistcoats were worn.

In the 1820s waistcoats became slightly longer with points in the front, known as the 'Hussar cut'. The rolled collar and lapel had no notch between but formed a rolled border which ended at the second or third button. However, the most popular collar style was still a stand collar but was lower than previously. They were mainly single-breasted although double-breasted waistcoats with a roll collar were popular for morning wear. The rolled collar could be of a different coloured material to give the impression of an under-waistcoat. For evening wear the collar could be notched or continue with the lapel. This latter style was called 'en schal' or a shawl collar.

Waistcoats usually had two pockets, one either side low down and occasionally one higher up on the left, crescent shaped to hold a pocket watch. For evening wear waistcoats were always single-breasted and white.

To help keep a good shape they were often tied with

tapes at the back, or fastened with a buckle and strap. The back of the waistcoat was usually of the same material as the lining, as it was cheaper and the back was not visible.

UNDER-WAISTCOATS

Under-waistcoats could be worn for warmth as an under-garment and usually had sleeves. Early in the 1800s the ornamental under-waistcoat consisted of just pieces of material joined to the back at the neck which protruded slightly from the over-waistcoat. When it became a complete garment, a stand collar was attached. Towards the end of the 1820s the parts visible around the over-waistcoat became more ornate and the protruding lapels were also of a contrasting colour.

By about 1828 two under-waistcoats could be worn, and when the over-waistcoat was left open to reveal the under-waistcoats, they were extremely ornate, often in white or sometimes quilted with decorative buttons. These waistcoats became so decorative and extravagant in style that it was difficult to recognise them from the upper waistcoats except that they were shorter.

LEGWEAR

Breeches were worn for evening wear until about 1810, and for day wear until about 1830 (but by the unfashionable until the end of the century) and were usually of a lighter colour than the rest of the suit. For sport, such as riding and hunting they were worn throughout the century and could also be made of leather and known as 'small-clothes' from about 1830. The front of the breeches opened with a flap known as a 'fall' with the fly front opening only used for evening wear and then only from the 1840s.

A band known as a 'bearer' — 'Bilston bearer' when deep or 'French bearer' when narrow — reached from one side to the other behind the flap or fall, buttoning across, and was worn to give support to the breeches. In the first decade of the century they were high waisted and fairly full at the hips. They were worn for evening wear until about 1810 and fastened at the knees or just beneath with either buttons or a buckle. After about 1824 the back of the breeches were tightened at the waist with a strap and buckle.

Until the 1820s there was one braces' button each side of the front, and by the 1830s breeches usually had two braces' buttons each side. The fall was made so that it was

Close-fitting double-breasted coat with large lapels. Tight-fitting ankle length pantaloons of cloth or stockinette were popular, c. 1832

wider below than towards the waist, to ensure a better fit.

Pantaloons, made of a stretch material and similar to tights were close fitting and ended at the thighs. Until about 1810 they were made with just one seam on the outside of the leg, after which they were also seamed on the inside. After about 1817 pantaloons reached the ankles and were open at the bottom and closed with either a running string or buttons and a strap under the instep to hold them taut. They had a waistband, the back having a vent and the front a small fall (until about 1825) when a fly opening was also used. There were also buttons present for the braces to be attached.

Pantaloons were worn mainly with Hessian or half-boots as well as Hussar buskins (calf-length boots). 'Moschettos', a variation with extensions similar to gaiters extending over the foot and strapped under the shoes, was also popular until about 1830. 'Wellington' pantaloons worn from about 1818 had side slits from the calf which were closed with buttons and loops.

Pantaloon trousers were not as tight fitting, and so did not have the side slits but they did have a strap passing under the foot to hold them down. Beau Brummel started the fashion for wearing black pantaloons with the straps worn beneath stockings under the foot for evening wear. They were buttoned tight to the ankles to give a smooth fit.

Trousers were first worn only for informal attire in about 1807 and for formal and evening wear from about 1817. They were not as close fitting as the pantaloons and ended just above the ankles, and were almost straight all the way down. There was sometimes a slit at the ankles. They were often made of a striped material and were worn with shoes, but could also be worn with gaiters.

By about 1817 trousers were longer, reaching the shoes and had straps passing under the foot which were attached to buttons either side inside the bottom of the trousers. They had a waistband, quite wide (until about 1830) with a braided edge. Until about 1823 the fall opening was used.

Trouser pockets, when fly fronts were used, were always inserted vertically into the side seams. At the back the trousers were tightened by means of a vent which was pulled in by a strap buckle.

Braces were attached by buttons one at each side of the front and the same at the back until about 1825. Thereafter two each side in front. The buttons were mainly made of metal or bone.

In 1814, when the Czar of Russia visited England he created a fashion for a type of trouser known as 'Cossacks'. They were full cut, gathered at the waist and ankles, but from about 1820 the fullness was pleated at the waist and the ankles were pulled in by a running string or ribbon. Although popular until mid-century, they became less voluminous in the 1830s.

orientale

NECKWEAR

Neckwear was an important supplement to men's fashion, especially in the first half of the century. Coat collars were not as high as they had been. Shirt collars were turned up high with two points extending to the cheeks, or else turned down over the stock or cravat. By 1815 the collar was so high that neckcloths became wider and were starched or stiffened.

In the 1820s shirt collars could be separate and kept on with ribbon ties which fastened at the back

The *cravat* was a large square or triangle of either lawn, muslin or silk, often starched, and worn around the neck, the ends tied in a bow or knot at the front. For informal wear, cravats could be coloured or patterned, but for formal wear they were almost always plain white and from about 1818 they had such names as the 'American' (of striped material and starched, worn with a stiffener), 'Ballroom' (in white and only slightly starched), an unstarched style known as the 'Byron' and the 'Gastronomic' (unstarched, worn with a stiffener, the knot being elastic to allow for loosening if required). In the 1830s very large cravats known as 'scarves' were worn round the shirt collar and spread over the shirt front and fastened with a tie pin. Very small cravats, first worn in the 1830s became extremely fashionable in the 1840s.

The *stock* was a shaped, made-up, stiffened neckband, fastened at the back with ties, buckles or hooks-and-eyes. It was made of a stiff material or horsehair and covered with either satin or velvet, and was worn high. Stocks were always popular military wear, but they became a civilian fashion about 1822, when a full-dress stock of black velvet with a satin bow was named after George IV.

For informal wear, a style called a 'Plain Bow' was of black silk with a plain bow in the front. Another style

Primo Tempo

Irlandaise

A la Byron

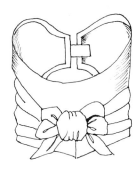

Royal George stock. c. 1830

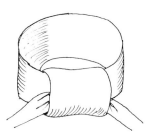

Wide cravat knot. c. 1830

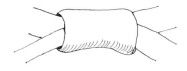

Military stock or a l'Americaine

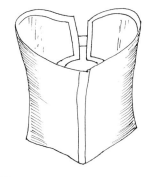

Silk mounted on to a leather shaped stiffener. c. 1830

Types of neckwear worn in the first part of the nineteenth century

was known as the 'Military' and was of black corded silk edged in soft leather and lined with red material. It was plain in front without a bow, and was fastened at the back with hooks-and-eyes.

OUTDOOR GARMENTS

At the beginning of the nineteenth century *greatcoats* or overcoats were voluminous, reaching the knees or ankles. They were usually single-breasted, buttoning to just beneath the waistline with either material or leather covered or mother-of-pearl buttons. The collar was high at the back, becoming lower towards the front. It joined the lapels with a V or M notch. The back of the coat had either a vent or tack-over (see Glossary) — a slight overlap or pleat. The front skirts were straight with a pleat in the sides. The shoulder and side seams were towards the back similar to that on a dress coat. The coat could have flapped hip pockets, but it was more usual to have breast pockets, usually on the inside.

After the first decade the coat was sometimes fastened with three to four straps as well as the buttons. It became calf length with collar, lapels and cuffs often fur trimmed, but if the collar was of the stand type it could also be fur lined, and turned down if so required. This particular style did not have lapels. The pockets were usually flapped. By the 1820s the coat, either single- or double-breasted often almost reached the ankles. The deep roll collar, often fur lined, could be worn with or without lapels. The buttons became quite large. There were waist pockets with flaps, but also popular were the pockets in the pleats at the sides. The sleeves became 'en gigot', gathered at the shoulders, and the cuffs were often buttoned on the outside. The back of the coat had a vent and there were also pleats at the sides. In the 1830s the collar became high and wide with a turn-over lined with fur and worn with or without lapels. The length varied and could reach to just below knee level. There were pockets in the skirts, concealed by the pleats.

Another style, a loose 'box coat' could be belted or the back fullness could be held in with a strap. The front fastening was usually with buttons or tabs. Various shoulder capes were a distinguishing feature of the coats which were originally worn on the box of a coach as a driving coat. In inclement weather the coat was also worn for walking.

A light, fitted coat from 1818 was known as a 'demi-surtout' and its bigger brother, the surtout greatcoat, was a fitted coat similar to a frock coat.

There were several versions of greatcoats from the 1830s, a military greatcoat which was usually double-breasted with Brandenburg fastenings (see Glossary) was of material with collar and lapels edged in silk.

The 'Polish' greatcoat fastened with loops and frogs and was long and close fitting, the collar, lapels and cuffs faced with lambskin, and the coat silk lined. It could also be worn for evening wear and was popular from about 1810.

The growing popularity of waterproof outdoor garments began from about 1823 when Charles Macintosh patented a waterproof fabric named after him. This weatherproof material was used in a variety of coat styles.

The 'pilot' coat which appeared about 1830, single- or double-breasted, was a loose and casual coat ending just above knee level. The collar ends were round and faced with either velvet or silk quilting. Sometimes it had only side seams, the loose back being without pleats or vent. Pockets could be set at a slant or have flaps.

The 'paletot', also single- or double-breasted worn instead of a frock coat from about 1835, was similar to a short great coat. The collar was small with a lapel. The coat was not seamed at the waist, and could be worn loose or fitted with a seam down the centre back.

The 'Taglioni' greatcoat, a double-breasted style, had a large collar and lapels faced with velvet or silk. The short full skirts did not have any pleats, but the seam at the waist was only in the front with vertical slit pockets at hip level. The cuffs on the sleeves were turned back.

Along with a great number of coats, the 'Petersham' greatcoat had a shoulder cape and a spreading collar.

A 'spencer' was a short, waisted jacket with long sleeves ending in round cuffs. The jacket was like a morning coat without tails and was worn over a tail coat when out-of-doors. It was very much a Regency fashion and worn only by the elderly after *c.* 1840.

Cloaks, although not very fashionable, were still worn for travelling, and were long and voluminous with slits sometimes covered with flaps, for the arms to protrude. The cloaks were long and usually fastened down the front with flaps. For evening wear they could have a large fur collar or have sleeves and a square collar with a deep cape

Long to the ankle redingote, with full skirts. The large collar often being fur or velvet. Double waistcoats were worn for extra warmth. Close-fitting pantaloons which reached the ankle were very fashionable and were made often in jersey and were comfortable and warm, c. 1830

Cloaks were very popular and were worn with and without sleeves. A shoulder cape was attached, c. 1829

with buttoning and a waist girdle.

By the 1830s travelling shoulder *capes* were shaped to fit the shoulders and neckline, with a large turned-down collar. They could also have detachable shoulder capes.

Opera cloaks were very full with a roll collar and perhaps a short cape.

Shawls were worn over coats for travelling from about 1820.

FORMAL WEAR

For Court wear the *dress coat* was usually single-breasted with the front panels curved towards the back. The most popular material was velvet which could be embroidered; dark greens, browns and blues were the most popular colours. Breeches could be of either velvet or silk and edged with lace. Waistcoats were of white satin, whilst stockings of white silk were worn with black buckled shoes. A bag wig (see Glossary) was invariably worn and a chapeau bras (see Glossary) carried.

For full evening dress the coat could be single- or double-breasted, the buttons either in gilt or covered in the coat's material. Pockets were in the pleats and pocket flaps were placed over sham ones. Waistcoats of velvet, satin or silk, stockings in white and kerseymere (see Glossary) breeches were in white or a pale natural colour were worn until trousers and pantaloons came into fashion in the 1830s. Buckled shoes or pumps were worn.

For weddings the dress coat was worn with gilt buttons. The white waistcoat could be of velvet and the underwaistcoat quilted. The breeches or pantaloons were often buff or pale coloured. Stockings were of silk, worn with buckled shoes or pumps. The shirts were frilled and ruffled, the cravat or neckerchief could be fastened with a jewelled pin. Dress gloves were a popular accessory.

INFORMAL WEAR

A dressing or *morning gown*, sometimes of silk or rich brocades, was worn indoors instead of a coat, and was popularly worn in the mornings. It hung loosely, wrapping over in the front and tied around the waist with a cord. Often a tasselled skull cap and slippers were also worn. For men who used powder on their wigs, *powdering gowns*, similar to the dressing gown were worn.

In the 1820s morning gowns could be of lined chintz

or cotton worn with a striped or coloured shirt. A *banyan*, another type of morning attire, was slightly waisted and could have a vent or pleat at the back with hip buttons.

By the 1830s *dressing gowns* were often patterned and brightly coloured and could be of cashmere, a type of woollen material, or of Indian silk.

For riding, frock coats, pantaloons, sometimes in white or of doeskin, were worn with Hessian boots, or alternatively, breeches with top boots. Tall hats were the usual headwear. From about 1825 a riding coat called a *Newmarket* from 1838, was popular. This coat is already described under the 'coat' section (see page 8). It could be single or double-breasted with tight sleeves and a low, flat collar, and was worn with breeches or tight trousers. A hard topped hat was worn for riding. For hunting the coat was like a short frock coat with deep flapped waist pockets, as well as two hip pockets on the inside large enough to hold a hare or rabbit. Strapped trousers and half-boots were worn as well as a buff-coloured top hat. After about 1830 the short frock coat could also be double-breasted, with two breast pockets as well as large flapped ones on the hips which were used as well as breast ones. The buttons were often decorated with hunting designs. Breeches, top boots and gaiters were worn. For headwear, top hats or jockey caps were popular.

A short frock coat usually single-breasted worn for shooting, until the 1830s had a turned down collar without lapels. The frock had many pockets: flapped waist pockets, a flapped breast pocket as well as two hip pockets on the inside large enough to hold game. After about 1830 the short frock coat could also be double-breasted, with two breast pockets as well as large flapped ones on the hips which were closed with buttons, and two very large ones in the skirt linings to take game. For yachting and boating, loose trousers and a white chip hat were very popular. A cravat fashionable for these activities was of checked cloth worn loosely round the neck.

FOOTWEAR

Boots were very fashionable in the first part of the century and were often named after famous people such as Wellington and Napoleon. These were of a military style made of black calfskin to knee height with a slightly lower back to allow the knee to bend. Spurs were worn by men of fashion on all occasions, even when not riding. Riding boots known as

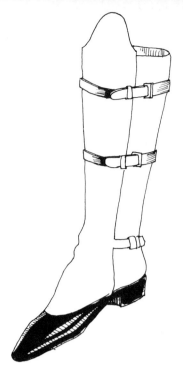

Leather galliskin with buckle and straps. c. 1815

Top boot with large turn down, usually of a different colour. c. 1820

High boot in a soft leather for walking. c. 1814

Wellington breeches over boots. c. 1820

'*military long boots*' were quite high in front, but low at the back. *Top boots* were slightly lower ending below the knees and had, as their name implies, turned-down tops, often in a lighter colour. Loops on each side facilitated pulling on the boots which could be held up by 'boot garters' attached to the back of the boot and fastened above the knees. These boots were usually worn with breeches and had low square heels and rounded toes.

Hessians, named after the boots of the soldiers of Hesse in Germany and still popular from the previous century, were short riding boots, close fitting to just below the knees with the fronts slightly peaked and often decorated with a tassel. The toes were slightly squared.

Buskins or hussar boots were similar, only shorter and did not have tassels at the points. There were also worn with pantaloons as were the Hessians.

Another type of boot still worn were *highlows*, popular amongst the working class. These were calf length and laced up the front. They were made of calfskin and were sometimes lined with sealskin.

Short boots were worn only out of doors. Ankle boots were close fitting with slits at the sides to make them easier to put on. A type of Wellington boot worn under trousers or pantaloons in the 1830s was made for evening wear.

Wellington boots, which were similar to top boots, became fashionable about 1819.

Bluchers, a type of half-boot, named after the commander of the Prussian army at Waterloo, were popular in the 1820s; they were open in the front and fastened over a tongue. Towards the end of this decade pointed toes came into fashion and high heels were gaining in popularity.

In 1839 vulcanized rubber was patented and was used for heels and soles of boots and shoes as well as for sports shoes with canvas uppers. Elastic-sided boots also made their appearance with their gussets of rubber set in either side.

After the French Revolution in 1789, *buckles* on shoes became unfashionable and were replaced by laces, in spite of a protest by British bucklemakers who had petitioned the Prince of Wales to help keep them in fashion. Shoes which had rounded toes and low heels were tied with latchets or straps over a fairly large tongue.

For Court wear shoes had short toe caps and were decorated with ribbon ties or, occasionally, buckles. These shoes were sometimes referred to as 'slippers'. Pumps or dress shoes of Spanish leather were always worn for formal occasions. A specially treated leather which was varnished and lacquered until it shone — *patent leather* — began to be used in the first quarter of the century. This type of leather was used mainly for footwear intended for Court or dress occasions, as well as dancing.

The working classes, concerned, above all, with practicality in clothes, wore hard-wearing leather shoes with thick soles studded with nails. *Spatterdashes* (see Glossary) or gaiters reached just below knee level and buttoned on the outer side. They were mainly worn in the country with breeches and were made of cloth.

Half-gaiters were shorter and just reached above the ankles. These were worn with pantaloons or trousers if shoes instead of boots were worn. *Stockings* could be made of a variety of materials such as cotton, wool or silk. For Court wear they were usually in white with clocks (see Glossary), whilst for evening wear they could be flesh coloured in open work and embroidered. In winter understockings could also be worn for warmth. By 1820 ribbed stockings were popular. Half-stockings, another name for socks, were usually worn with a negligee.

Soft elastic sided boot with leather toe piece. c. 1837

HAIRSTYLES

Short queued (see Glossary) wigs as well as ordinary wigs, following popular hairstyles, were worn by the older or professional men, that is legal and churchmen, but the trend of wearing wigs became less favoured because of a tax on hair powders introduced in 1795. Fashionable hairstyles had an untidy and dishevelled look, known as *à la Titus,* or the *Brutus crop* which was a shorter version. During the second decade of the nineteenth century hair was long enough to be curled and waved and the dishevelled look fell from favour.

After about 1810 men allowed their hair to grow longer with curls and waves becoming fashionable. Closely curled hair was particularly popular. Centre or side partings were worn. The back hair was cut shorter as this was more practical with high collars. Hair could be brushed forward from the crown, and loose waves were permitted to fall across the forehead.

The face was clean shaven but, following the military style, side-whiskers could be worn. By about 1825 there was

Spat shoe with buttoning on the side

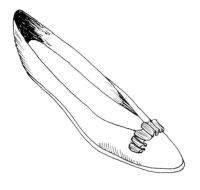

Kid leather slipper shoe

c. 1823

c. 1830

c 1834

c. 1840

a new mode of whiskers and beard which met under the chin and formed a frame around the face. By about 1829 the *favourite*, a small tuft of hair beneath the chin, became popular.

The beginning of the nineteenth century saw the introduction of a number of hair-care products such as *macassar oil* which became so popular that '*anti-macassars*' (or ornamented coverings for chair and sofa backs) became necessary as well as fashionable. *Moustache wax*, a mixture of beeswax and pomade, helped stiffen and keep in shape the moustaches. There were various dyes and colourants on the market as well as several aids to help hair grow and prevent it from falling out.

Until about 1820 children usually had their hair dressed short and simply. Small boys wore their hair in long curls from the 1830s, but when they were older it was cut shorter.

HEADWEAR

Hats were varied in the early part of the century. Some had low, flat crowns with wide brims curved at the sides. These were mainly worn in the country and were also popular with the elderly or were worn for informal wear by the unfashionable. Some had bowl-shaped crowns with narrower brims curved up at the sides, and were similar to the later bowler hats.

Top hats had tall crowns with the brim turned down front and back, also known as *toppers* they were perhaps the single most popular style with several variations. The *Wellington hat*, one type typical of the 1820s, had the crown curving out towards the top, and the narrow brim turned up all round. A tall cylindrical hat had the brim turned up at the sides only. Another style, called the *turf*, had a tapering medium high crown with a brim that was wider and curved up acutely at the sides.

Opera hats, always in black material or beaver, sometimes decorated with feathers and a tassel front and back, were also known as *cocked* hats, *chapeau bras* or *military folding* hats. The crescent-shaped soft crown was hidden by the rather high front and back brims or peaks which could be folded, thus making it possible for the hat to be carried under the arm. These were usually worn or carried on formal occasions.

In 1812 a hat for semi-formal occasions was patented called an *elastic round hat*, a predecessor to the folding

Top hat with narrow turned up brim. c. 1819

LEFT: *Gentleman in informal dress, a cut-away square-ended coat with tails. The pantaloons were close fitting to the legs and were strapped under the shoes, c.1803.*
CENTRE: *Lady wearing a high waisted style dress over which is the short spencer with its high-standing collar and long sleeves fur trimmed at the wrist. She is also carrying a beaded bag with tassels.*
RIGHT: *Lady wearing the classical high waisted Empire style chemise gown with a low decolletage. Her silk bonnet hat is decorated with ribbon. An embroidered shawl is also carried.*

LEFT: *Boy dressed in a short jacket with a ribboned sash and close-fitting pantaloons with short hessian boots or buskins. He is wearing a peaked military type forage cap, 1810.*

CENTRE: *The lady is wearing the chemise gown popular in the Regency period, flimsy and lightweight. Over the shoulders is worn a shawl, c.1810.*

RIGHT: *Man in a tail coat and the looser type cossack trousers. Over the shoulder was worn a voluminous Leblanc cloak. A beaver type of top hat is also worn.*

Silk covered top hat. c. 1840

Top hat in light coloured material. c. 1840

Low crowned round hat with wide turned up brim. c. 1819

opera hat. This hat, made of either beaver or silk, was stiffened as other hats, apart from the middle part of the crown which was fitted with an elastic steel spring, 7-10cm long and sewn either side inside the crown so that the hat could be flattened when so required. By about 1830 the 'elastic hat' was losing its popularity and was superseded by a *circum-folding dress hat* which was a softer style, round in shape.

Tall hats could have vertical sides and flat crowns with a narrow brim turned up at the sides, or the sides could taper towards the top rather like an inverted flower pot. Tall hats with the top widening, the reverse of the previous style gained in popularity about 1819 and became very fashionable in the following decade. They had various names: the *Cumberland* or *à la William Tell* which was about 20 cm tall tapering, with a narrow brim turned up at the sides. This was also often alluded to as a pointed hat, and was very fashionable from about 1830-37.

Zero hats had upright crowns and with slight variations were known as the Aylesbury, Oxonian, Tilbury etc.

Very small flat hats were fashionable for a short while amongst the dandies. Hats were blocked in a round shape until 1817, and instead of having to use a hat-screw to stretch the hat to fit, a new method was introduced which could produce an oval shape to fit the head.

Caps were worn for horse riding and had stiff crowns with a peak in the front. When worn for travelling they were quite plain and resembled skull caps. By the late 1830s quartered caps with a band and sometimes also a peak were worn by schoolboys.

BEAUTY AIDS

Fashionable gentlemen blanched the backs of their hands and coloured their cheeks with either walnut juice or rouge. They also wore, early in the century, a type of corset called an 'Apollo', which was similar to a lady's, made of whalebone, to make their waists smaller and puff out their chests.

ACCESSORIES

Gloves were made of leather or cotton for day wear, and from about 1829 evening gloves were made of white silk as well as kid leather. By the early 1840s gloves became an important accessory, doeskin being very popular for riding. They were usually in pale colours, whilst for evening wear white or buff-coloured kid was popular as well as silk.

Wrist muffs, known as 'muffatees', made of knitted worsted, were worn from the late 1820s. *Canes* were popular and could be of ebony with a gold or ornamented head. The handle could be of carved ivory or ebony, and they almost always had strings and tassels attached.

Umbrellas also became popular with ornamented handles. Beau Brummel carried a cane or an umbrella with a sheath covering of silk material. Rings, shirt brooches, seals hanging from fobs and cravat pins were amongst the fashionable jewellery worn. Snuff boxes, gold watches and chains were also worn, as well as quizzing glasses. Shirt buttons could be jewelled and encircled in gold whilst pocket handkerchiefs were usually scented and made of either silk or cotton. From the 1830s shirts were an impressive part of clothing. They were profusely frilled, embroidered, gathered or pleated.

Double-breasted cut-away coat with buttoned at the wrist sleeves. Single-breasted waistcoat. Long to the ankle pantaloons in a nankeen material. A large-brimmed top hat was very fashionable, c. 1818

Women

DRESSES

By 1790 dresses began to have higher waistlines, being at their highest about 1805. The long skirts were of a semi-transparent material revealing pantaloons beneath. Both day and evening dresses were similar (except for the trimmings which were more ornate for evening wear) and could be trained with low necklines and long or short sleeves. These classical styles which began in the late 1790s had classical ornamentations as well as Egyptian and Gothic. The classical styles were particularly suited to young ladies, whilst the Gothic style, from about the 1820s, also suited older women. The flowing classical lines became more shaped when soft muslins were superseded by more solid materials. In the 1830s the angular lines reached their peak with extensions at the top of the dress and the base forming two triangles, the points meeting at the waist. In the late 1830s the silhouette again became softer.

The *round robe* was a combination of a full loose chemise and the robe à l'anglaise, a sack back gown with pleats sewn to waist level. It was sometimes made without a waist seam, but could be high waisted and very full. The seams at the back of the bodice were all set so far back to give the appearance of a very small back. The sleeves were also set far in. The front of the bodice could be gathered at the neck and waistline or it could be fitted with a V-shaped neckline filled in with a fichu (see Glossary), or have a cross-over front. The skirt was full gathered in front with the back usually in box pleats worn over pads. The fitted sleeves could be any length.

The Greek influence, dating from the 1790s, introduced a dress originating from the chemise but longer and fuller with a drawstring at the neckline and also just below the breast giving the impression of a high waistline. Gradually the neckline became lower and the train at the back longer, but the train could be looped up by a cord suspended from the back of the shoulder. This was known as the *Empire gown* and was made of a diaphanous material.

Another style of dress had a close-fitting bodice with a low décolletage. The skirt front was straight with a slight gathering at the sides to fit over the hips. The back could be full to allow for freer movement, or else the side seams could have a slit. Occasionally an overtunic could be worn. These Greek-style dresses were almost always trained.

Until about 1810 there was a bib or apron-fronted robe. The bodice back and the side fronts were lined, with the front flaps fastened crosswise to act as a brassière The skirt was attached to the bodice at the back with a slit at the sides. The front of the bodice sewn to the skirt had tapes either side at waist level. With the apron front in position, the tapes were tied at the back, sometimes under the skirt. The top was pinned to the shoulders. For informal wear the bodice could be high necked or, if low, filled in with a chemisette (see Glossary) or habit-shirt. The bodice material was often cut on the cross to make it more clinging.

Another gown, either round or trained, was fastened with a 'fall' in the front part of the skirt. The upper front portion of the skirt was open at the side seams forming placket (pocket) holes. The top of this flap was gathered at the waistline on to a band and tied like an apron, either over or under the bodice which could be a cross over, like a shawl, or have the two front parts joined with lacing and worn over a fill-in, 'habit-shirt' or chemisette. The waistcoat bosom was closed by buttons. This was known as a *Cottage front*. Both these bodice styles were for day wear only.

Another style of stomacher-front gown had the bodice sewn to the skirt flap, like an apron bib, which was then attached to a shoulder strap with pins or buttons. An under-bodice worn beneath the bib front was attached to the lining. This type of bodice usually had a low décolletage, and the backs of these bodice styles appeared narrow shouldered due to the deep-set sleeves. The back of the skirts were given a slight bustle effect with the insertion of a padded roll attached at the back part of the skirt. The frock, skirt and

Ladies in the Empire style with a high waisted round gown reaching
the ankles, the bodice and skirt in one. Both narrow and deep ruffs
were worn around the neck. c. 1806

bodice in one, was usually fastened at the back with buttons until about 1810 when hooks-and-eyes became more popular The untrained dress with bodice and skirt cut as one was fastened at the back.

The dress could have a high standing collar ending in a small neck ruff or frills. The décolletage could also be low, either square or V-shaped with a fill-in called either a chemisette, habit-shirt or tucker (see Glossary). The bodice could also be 'à l'enfant' which was a rounded neckline gathered by a running string. Another type of day dress was fastened down the entire front with buttons and known as a chemise robe. The bodice usually had a ruff around the neck (1820s) or it could be vandyked. Skirts were slightly gored which enabled them to be fuller without needing to be gathered. Bustles could be worn under the skirt high at the waist to give a 'Grecian band' effect. To give a small waist Apollo corsets were worn. The hems of the skirts often ended with flounces or could be vandyked to match the bodice neckline.

From the 1820s the shoulder line of the bodice widened and puffed sleeves gave a broad shape to the top of the body which was balanced with a full skirt at its base. This accentuated the fashionable small waist and was now lower towards the natural waist level which also facilitated tight lacing. The centre front could be slightly pointed from about 1833.

From about 1836 the general silhouette altered, shoulders becoming narrow and sloped; sleeves became less enormous and the waistline became longer, buckled belts also became popular. Separate bodice and skirts did not become popular attire until about 1818.

DAY DRESSES
From the second decade of the nineteenth century the dress bodice was divided into two main types, at least until the 1840s. If the front was close fitting, the material was cut on the cross and fitted with darts from the breasts to the centre front at the waist. If the bodice was loose fitting it was gathered with the fullness equally spread around the neckline, but at the waist the fullness was towards the centre front. This style was cut from straight material. The back was always cut on the straight in two pieces joined down the centre and the side seams from the armholes were curved in the back to give a slender appearance. Shoulder seams also tended to be further back to give an elegant look.

Sleeves could be short, puffed, cut on the cross and worn

Ladies in day dresses with wide demi-gigot sleeves over which lay large pelerine. Both bertha collars and boas of tulle were worn. The ankle length skirt was fully gathered at the waist and extended with petticoats. Bonnets were wide and made of straw or silk and decorated with ribbons and flowers

over longer sleeves. If they were long they could be caught in puffs all the way down by ribbons and known as 'Marie sleeves'. After about 1820 the tops of sleeves expanded and flounced, ornate epaulettes known as 'mancherons' were worn, especially with the puffed-at-the-shoulder sleeves which came tight to the wrists and ended in ruffles. The 'demi-gigot' type sleeve was full at the top, becoming tighter at the elbows and then close fitting to the wrists, sometimes extending over the hands. The gigot sleeve, also known as 'leg-of-mutton', worn from about 1825, was extremely large from the shoulders, diminishing to just below the elbow and then close to the wrists. These sleeves were cut on the cross with the top cut in a circular shape and gathered at the shoulder. An 'Imbecile' sleeve was full all the way down to the wrist and then gathered to a close-fitting cuff. The fullness in the sleeves was achieved with either padding or stiff buckram lining — even whalebone hoops were used. Long, transparent sleeves were worn over short, puffed sleeves for evening wear.

Until about 1828 *skirts* were ground length after which they became shorter, just reaching the ankles. They were always gored, the angles becoming more acute as the skirts became fuller. For simple dresses they were cut in two parts with the front gored; the centre back, however, was always plain. The seams were sewn so that the gored part was sewn to the straight of the material, and the skirt clung to the body in front, but the back was full. When skirts were made in soft materials such as silk, the seams were sewn gore to gore. As with soft materials it is difficult to sew material on the cross to a straight piece without it puckering. When skirts became much fuller they were either pleated or gathered at the waist. As the bottom of the skirts became wider, the hem was padded with cotton wool. This method was popular from the early 1820s. The skirts from hem to knee level were decorated with a profusion of trimmings.

A *round gown*, at the turn of the century, was a gown without a train, but the old meaning of a slightly trained overgown with bodice and skirt joined and closed remained in vogue until about 1806. After about 1810 Classical lines were beginning to be superseded by a more Gothic style of trimming.

Gores — wedge-shaped pieces of material — were used in the construction of bodices and skirts, the skirts also being slightly gathered from the waist, which gradually was lowered

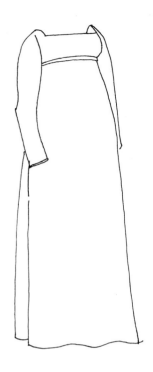

Empire line, waisted dress usually of white muslin c. 1806

to the natural level after about 1820. The skirts were mainly worn to ankle length and without trains. They could be made separately from the bodice which was closed in front, whilst the skirt had a back fastening. This style was known as 'jacket and petticoat'. The jacket usually had a neck ruff and the skirt was decorated with vandyked flounces.

Between 1820 and the 1830s the *round dress* fastened at the back. The bodice could have a small turn-down collar or frill high at the neck or if low, it was called a bodice 'à l'enfant'. The gathering on the band could end in revers which spread over the shoulders, cape-like. A bodice ending in a point at the waist was draped across the front and could be pleated from shoulders to waist. Fichu robings or pelerine (see Glossary) lapels were revers on V-shaped décolletages and converged from the shoulders to the waist.

Pelerine robes, originating from the pelisse (see Glossary), were similar to dresses fastening down the front or towards the side by hidden hooks-and-eyes which could be covered by decorative bows. Around 1825 a pelisse robe called a *redingote* had a large flat collar with a tight fitting bodice and was worn mainly for walking out. Around the waistline a belt with a buckle or a sash could be worn.

About 1836 the silhouette changed from wide shoulders and sleeves, small waist and full skirt to a softer shape with smaller sleeves and sloping shoulders. Bodices became close fitting and if they were not pointed at the waist, belts with buckles were usually worn.

The new shapes of sleeves (like the 'bishop sleeve') were not as stiff in appearance, although they were full from the shoulders, gathered at the wrists into a closed cuff. They were made of a softer material and not padded. Another soft style was the sleeve *en bouffant* which could be puffed at intervals with tight bands. Mancherons were popular until the 1820s. They were an oversleeve, short and ungathered, falling over dress sleeves, gradually becoming more like epaulettes which were decorative shoulder pieces.

Until about 1836 skirts reached the ankles after which they reached almost to the ground. They were either gathered or pleated to the waist with placket hole openings. Pockets were tied around the waist beneath the skirt.

Skirt decoration had previously been up the entire skirt, but with the fullness fashionable from about 1830 trimmings now were only to about knee level, consisting of appliquéed patterns and embroidered hems. After about 1836 flounces

Dome-shaped day dress with several stiff petticoats. c. 1840

were also popular around the base of the skirts, as well as skirts *en tablier* — trimmings either side from the waist down to give the appearance of an apron in the front.

For evening wear a *trained gown*, similar to the eighteenth-century style, was worn open in front revealing the lavishly ornamented petticoat which was part of the garment and not worn as underwear.

Sleeves for most dresses, if long, were usually not too tight fitting and reached over the hand from a wrist band. Short oversleeves were quite usual, although short sleeves themselves could also be worn.

For evenings a *tunic dress* (worn with an underdress either trained or round) accompanied a tunic which could hang loosely from the shoulders or was tied around the waist, the hem not always being even. This was worn mainly in the first decade. In the 1830s a tunic dress with the over-skirt in a diaphanous material and shorter than the under-skirt was worn with one side looped up with ribbon knots and artificial flowers.

In the 1820s the bodice of evening dresses mainly followed the style of those worn in the daytime, except that the décolletage was always low. The bodice *en coeur*, the front being heart-shaped with the point centre front, had narrow horizontal pleats around the edge. It was an off-the-shoulder style which, because of its tight fit, stayed up although it was not boned.

Sleeves which were short and puffed became more enlarged towards 1829 when they were cut in a circular shape and sometimes kept distended with whalebones. These were known as 'beret' sleeves similar to beret type hats. Long transparent oversleeves were also popular.

Evening skirts were shorter than those worn in the daytime, and they were more ornately ornamented at the hems. Striped material was quite fashionable.

In the 1830s the bodice, which was close fitting with an extremely low neckline, was often boned down the centre front. The décolletage was often covered with lace and ribbon bows decorating the front.

After about 1836 the beret-type sleeves (see Glossary) became smaller and less popular. A variation, however, still being worn had several bouffants or puffs to elbow level. Generally the sleeves were tight to the elbow and

Wedding dress with Marie sleeves. c. 1829

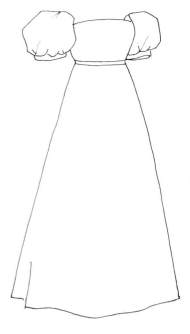

Evening dress worn over a boned corset. c. 1827

*Evening gown with gigot sleeves
c. 1836*

*Evening dress with a cape collar
and beret sleeves*

abundantly covered with lace ruffles or blond.

For semi-evening attire 'imbecile' sleeves were worn until about 1836. From that date ribbon knots were used a great deal on the shoulders and sleeves. Skirts, after 1836, were sometimes trained.

FORMAL WEAR

Hooped petticoats were necessary for Court wear until 1820 when George IV became king but were replaced by robes trained and draped over embroidered petticoats. A high ostrich feathered headdress as well as a tiara was very popular. Large white soft kid gloves were also worn. When the hoop became fashionable, the skirts remained trained, but could be held over the arm.

For mourning, black was the usual colour worn, although dark brown was also permissible. For weddings, dresses were often of lace over white satin. The skirts were trained and sleeves usually short, but long gloves were worn. A cottage bonnet with a lace veil pinned to the head was popular, or just a veil with a wreath of orange blossom was also fashionable. A white satin pelisse with swan's down trimming could be worn over a wedding dress.

INFORMAL WEAR

The *riding habit* was similar in cut to a robe, but with longer skirts. The bodice had short basques (see Glossary) at the sides and front, and had long sleeves with cuffs. The bodice could be double breasted or left open to reveal the habit shirt, the bodice also had a collar. The bodice and skirt were joined, sometimes only at the back, with the front like an apron-front skirt. The habit could be made in two parts. The riding costume was often ornamented down the front as well as on the cuffs. A black beaver hat decorated with cord and tassels as well as an occasional ostrich feather was worn, as were black half boots. Tan leather gloves completed the outfit. By the 1830s the bodice was often buttoned down the front with a falling collar, gigot sleeves, black stock, cloth pantaloons were worn beneath. The front of the bodice could be decorated with buttons whilst the collar and cuffs could be lace trimmed.

A specially designed *walking dress* appeared about 1802 and was untrained and ended just above ground level. The hem could be edged with small tucks which were later

Ladies in winter costumes with a natural waistline. The bonnets were large and sheltered the face and were decorated with feathers, fastening under the chin. c. 1818/19 The man's coat, known as a redingote was close fitting at the waist and was fastened with braid frogging. c. 1819

Lady in a riding costume with the sloping shoulders and long waistline. Worn under the skirt were long breeches which strapped under the boots. At the neckline was a stand collar with a stock tied in a bow. c. 1831

replaced by flounces and by about 1810 the skirt hem was often scalloped or vandyked. The sleeves were often in a different colour to the main body of the dress. Coloured stockings were worn with this attire.

OUTDOOR WEAR

A pelisse, also known as a *carriage dress,* was open down the front and was at first three-quarter length, later becoming longer to the ankles. It could also be lined with silk, satin or velvet. The neck was high and ended with two or more cape collars or a stand collar. The back of the gown could be cut without a waist seam and pleated to fit the waistline. Closure, if required, was by buttoning either to waist level, or from neck to bosom, or the complete length. The long sleeves were full to fit over those of the dress and could continue over the hand. Sleeves, which could also be full and puffed at the shoulders, often had epaulettes or mancherons (see Glossary) decorating the shoulder seam.

The *pelisse* was sometimes sleeveless, in which case it was more like a mantle with holes for the arms. At the back, on the inside, tapes could be attached which were then tied around the waist, the skirt part of the pelisse following the shape of the dress worn beneath. It was ornamented with trimmings to match the dress as well as with chevrons. The base could be padded in the hem.

The *spencer,* a short jacket worn over a bodice, of similar construction to the pelisse, was tight-fitting at the waist, reaching to just below knee level until about 1804. The jacket was fastened down the front with a V-shaped opening or a high-necked collar. For outdoor wear the sleeves were long, while for evenings the spencer could be sleeveless. These were popular until the 1820s. About 1814 a *spencer-ette* became fashionable, this was a close-fitting jacket closed over the bosom with a low neckline which was edged with a lace frill.

Cloaks and *mantles* were worn either three-quarter or full-length. The 'Witchoura' mantle had a long cape and was fur trimmed, popular until about 1818. In the 1830s the name was again used for a capeless mantle with a high stand collar and large hanging sleeves, again fur lined, as this was a mantle mainly worn in the winter. Other mantles, very voluminous, reached the skirt hems, and had large spreading collars or waistlength capes attached. Cloaks were very varied, some could have attached hoods. The

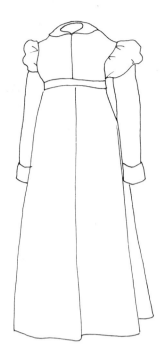

A pelisse for wearing over a dress. c. 1818

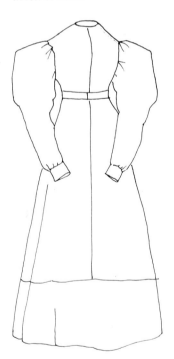

A pelisse-robe style dress with full sleeves

*Ladies in outdoor clothes of c. 1814. The gentleman is in close fitting
pantaloons and a square cut tail coat*

'curricle' cloak worn in the first few years of the century was half or three-quarter length, fitted to the waist and then sloping away, leaving the front exposed. It was trimmed with either lace or fur, depending upon the season. A mantlet worn as an outdoor cloak, sometimes known as a 'shawl' mantle was popular in the 1830s. It was a half shawl, shaped to the neckline with the points rounded. A hood or small cape could also be attached. Two other types of mantle were the 'Burnoise', a large, long mantlet with sometimes a hood worn mainly for evening attire and the 'pelerine' mantlet was an enlarged form of fichu-pelerine and had the cape part deep with the front strips wider and longer, but not caught under a belt.

Shawls, at the beginning of the century were usually not very large, but increased in size in the 1830s. 'Norwich' shawls were of silk and wool woven together with, sometimes, a Kashmir pattern. From about 1808 shawls of a paisley design were fashionable. Square shawls were being replaced by large silk scarves with the borders either brocaded or patterned from about 1809. By about 1814 shawls again became popular amongst older women. Indian shawls of worsted had a deep border on one side. French and other foreign shawls were imported after the Peace of Amiens in 1814 and were becoming larger, until they were about two metres square. They became quite fashionable again about 1835, being worn for travelling as well as for indoor wear. Fur tippets (short-shoulder capes) were worn in winter and were similar to a short shoulder cape.

Detachable laced undersleeves. c. 1840

Chemisette or fill-in. c. 1840

Five tiered betsie collorette of lace. c. 1807

*Padding worn around the arm
to distend the sleeves. c. 1830*

NECKWEAR

A *habit-shirt* or chemisette worn as a fill-in, was made in two parts joined around the waist with tapes and sewn together at the shoulders. It could have buttoning either front or back. A *tucker*, usually of lace, covered the décolletage, normally straight at the top and then shaped to fit into the neckline. *Neckerchiefs,* worn mainly with day dresses were knotted loosely in the front. A *tippet* made of lace or lawn had long streamers and was worn both for day and evening wear. If worn for the evening the tippet could be of swan's down. Coloured silk *cravats* were sometimes worn with ruffs, and gauze silk *scarves* were also popular. *Neck ruffs* ceased to be worn after about 1836 and turned-down collars became very broad. A *pelerine,* a cape-like flat collar, or a fichu-pelerine, was worn from about 1826. It was a shoulder covering wide enough to envelop large sleeves and droop over with them. It could consist of a double cape and turned-down collar, the ends of the fichu hanging down either side in the front and sometimes caught under the belt at the waist.

UNDERWEAR

The classical style of dress, still popular from the end of the previous century, meant that underwear worn with the thin muslin dresses was sparse. The only type of corset worn was a *zona,* a Greek type of brassière which was made of bands covered with silk or damask, wrapped around the upper part of the body and supporting the lower part of the breasts. Shoulder straps were added and it became more like a corset.

*Back laced corset in dimity
material. c. 1813*

Back laced corset. c. 1840

*Corset made in satin with
a laced fastening at the back.
c. 1835*

When the crinoline became fashionable it was fastened to the *corset* which was tightly laced at the waist, the top becoming like a modern brassière, having the breasts enclosed in separate cups. The corset also reached the top of the legs — the forerunner of the suspender belt.

Flesh coloured *drawers* had lace frills at the ankles which were sewn to the base of the long, wide linen or lawn trousers which were tied at the waist giving a fullness to the skirt. These trousers were often referred to as pantaloons or pantelettes. They became extremely popular about 1807.

Children still dressed as their elders, but little girls were permitted to discard the tight corsets, panniers and crinolines so that they could play with greater ease. However they still wore the lace trimmed pantaloons, especially when their dresses became shorter. Small boys also wore wider trousers than their fathers. Wax or cotton artificial bosoms were worn to give more shape to the upper part of the body.

In the decade from 1810 when classical lines were the vogue, *bustles* made in the shape of rolls were worn under the skirt, tied as high as possible beneath the skirts to help give the illusion of the Grecian shape. The bustle remained fashionable, becoming more important, especially with the tight lacing of corsets. They could be stiffened with cotton wadding to increase the size and were made with a crescent-shaped cushion tied around the waist, or could be tier upon tier of stiffened frills. *Demi-* or *half-corsets,* lightly boned with whalebone were worn for informal wear, whilst for more formal attire they were much longer and tightly laced, the tight lacing being a very important feature of the period, in order to give a small-waisted appearance.

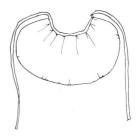

Tie-on back bustle. c. 1830

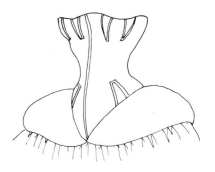

Pair of cushion panniers worn over a corset. c. 1840

FOOTWEAR

Ladies wore dainty and delicate shoes, tied with ribbons, made of satin and called 'bottines' and were in a material to match the dress. In the winter velvet, fur-lined boots were made which could be embroidered and fastened with ribbons. House and evening slippers were often made by the ladies themselves in delicate fabrics.

Flat-heeled shoes, which could be worn as slippers, had pointed toes and short uppers until about 1807 when the toes became more rounded. The toecaps were sometimes slashed so that the coloured linings could protrude. This was a brief revival of the Tudor fashion.

Ladies in fur trimmed winter mantles similar to the male redingote.
Muffs for extra warmth were carried c. 1827 and 1823. The gentleman
in the background is wearing an ankle length redingote with the full
sleeves tapered to the wrists. c. 1831

For evening wear rosettes were a popular form of decoration. Towards the end of the 1820s shoes and stockings almost always matched the day dresses in colour. An interest grew in the theatre and dance, flat ballet type shoes became extremely popular. About 1830 they were often worn with pink tights and black fishnet stockings over them to give the appearance of bare legs. These shoes had very waisted soles and little or no heels.

Shoes generally were greatly decorated in various ways. They could have intricately stitched designs on the uppers, or else be adorned with beading and embroidery. After the 1830s, in the Romantic era, heels became higher and shoes could be cut into open sandal shapes with two or three bows at the instep.

The fashion of wearing classical clothes and hairstyles brought also a revival of the Greek-type sandals with criss-crossed lacing up the legs of ribbon or leather thongs. By about 1806 (until 1815) sandals had wedge heels. Roman sandals were similar, also with criss-cross lacing tying up at the front.

Half boots worn for walking, known as 'high shoes', reached the calf and were laced leaving a slight gap to reveal the stockings. These boots could also be buttoned at the sides. A popular type about 1814 was the Wellington boot, named, needless to say, after the 'Iron Duke'. Insoles could be worn which were made of plaited horse hair and covered with velvet material. Silk half-boots were worn when travelling by carriage, and for evening wear they could be made of satin with pearls embroidered on them.

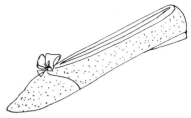

Heelless slipper shoe made in silk. c. 1815

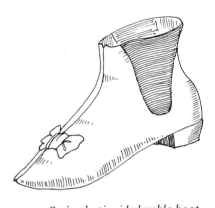

Satin elastic sided ankle boot. c. 1840

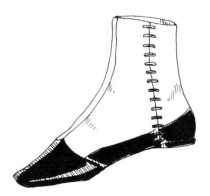

Satin ankle boot with side lacing, with leather toe cap and quarters. c. 1840

Low heeled slipper shoe of kid. c. 1812

By the 1830s when boots could be worn with gaiters of the same colour and material, they were laced and the gaiters buttoned. Boots were often worn with the uppers of a cloth material and the rest in leather and were fastened by lacing. Cloth boots could also be worn over slippers for the theatre. Boots of velvet, known as 'Adelaides', could be worn in winter, lined and trimmed with fur, when trimmed with fringes they were known as 'brodequins'. Black tassels were also popular as decoration on the insteps of boots and braid around the edges or front was also used a great deal. Highlows, a type of boot, were worn for country wear.

In the early part of the century pattens with wooden soles raised off the ground by metal rings were worn in inclement weather. Leather topped clogs with cork soles were also worn in bad weather.

Working women's shoes were of a sturdy type or clogs, which when worn for dress wear, were decorated and painted to look elegant. Stockings became an important feature as the dresses became semi-transparent, and were mainly in flesh colour. They were mainly made of wool, cotton or silk, in most colours, but pink was particularly popular. The material used for stockings was often of the same type as the dress. If not, they could be made of an openwork design in cotton. For balls and evening wear they were of silk and decorated with coloured clocks. In the mid 1830s they were usually black silk with cotton or lisle being worn in the daytime, mainly white or grey. Ribbed stockings with clocks came into fashion about 1815. Garters, when worn, were well below the knees.

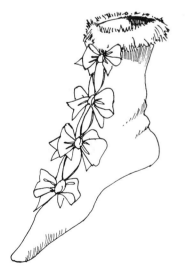

Fur edged boot with ribbon bow fastening. c. 1830

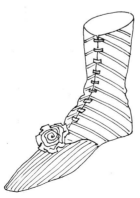

Silk bootee with rosette but without heels. c. 1820

Ballet type pumps tied over black net stockings c. 1836

Indoor *caps* had become less fashionable, small mob caps however being worn in the mornings or beneath hats. For formal occasions, however, a cap was necessary — mainly in the form of a turban. These were made in the same material as dresses, such as crêpe, muslin, lace, gold or silver net and other fine fabrics. For formal occasions they could be highly decorated with lace rosettes, gold net and aigrets intermixed, and arranged in a variety of ways.

Simple *turbans* or toques made of lamé trimmed with bird-of-paradise plumes were also popular especially at the opera. Toques were similar to turbans but more like a brimless hat. A beret or beret-turban, (quite large about 1827) worn at an angle and highly decorated with a variety of trimmings, became less popular as our period ended, about 1840.

Small round lace caps with ribbon trimmings rather than feathers and flowers were worn for morning dress, as well as lace or muslin veils or half-handkerchiefs draped over the head, especially in warmer weather.

Until the 1820s the shape of caps and turbans was oval, but as hairstyles became more elaborate, headwear had to follow in shape.

Caps were worn indoors in the daytime, mob caps and 'cornettes' for morning wear were made of embroidered muslin or trimmed lace. The mob cap was fairly large, gathered on to a band and could be tied under the chin with lappets. The biggin (see Glossary) was similar in style but without lappets. The cornette was shaped like a bonnet with a slight point at the back and tied under the chin. For evening wear they were made of a fine lace or crêpe and decorated with ribbons and flowers. A half-handkerchief was often decorated with flowers, with the point towards the back and the other two ends just allowed to hang down. A popular evening cap of lace could have a hole at the back to allow the bunches of curls at the back of the head to protrude.

In the late 1820s cornettes worn for morning wear made of a fine patterned lace with bows either of striped or checked ribbon. Small lace caps sometimes had coloured silk or tartan cauls, and from about 1827 the caps expanded in a mass of lace, ribbons and flowers.

Caps, although worn under bonnets, were seldom worn under hats. The elaborate coiffure caused the caps to have openings for the tall loops of hair, and by the middle of the 1830s long lappets were fashionable. Another style was

Mob cap gathered on to a band with the lappets tied under the chin. c. 1819

Pleated turban of transparent material. c. 1803

High crowned bonnet with a fastening under the chin. c. 1799

High crowned bonnets lavishly decorated and made from various
materials as well as straw.

high crowned and known as a 'babet' with a caul extending up and surrounded with flowers and ribbons. The cap itself had broad side trimmings and was flat on top.

Bonnets gradually increased in popularity. They were of the poke shape with the crown becoming higher about 1814 to accommodate tall hairstyles. They were made in an assortment of materials such as satin, crêpe, with velvet and straw the most popular.

Small cornettes were sometimes worn beneath bonnets, the frilled lace edge being visible. A 'bavolet' which was a frill at the back of the bonnet like a curtain, came into fashion about 1828 and lasted until the 1860s. The curves of the brim in front increased greatly early in the 1820s, so that wire or whalebone supports were required. The brims could also be lined with cardboard, especially if the bonnets were made of straw. These large bonnets had a profusion of ribbon bows and loops as well as flowers and feathers, and could be lined in the same material as the bonnet itself with an interlining of stiffer material. 'Mentonnières' or 'chin stays' were attached to these bonnets and formed a frill around the chin.

The 'capote' was a soft puffed-out crowned bonnet with a stiff brim projecting over the face. From about 1831 an oval-shaped brim with a high, almost perpendicular crown was popular and, instead of a cap worn beneath, decorations were placed on the underside of the brim as well.

The 'bibi' or 'cottage' bonnet was a smaller and simpler form, whilst the 'drawn' bonnet (similar to an eighteenth-century calash) was very fashionable about 1835 and was made of fine material such as silk and placed over a series of cane or whalebone hoops.

Large *veils* were often worn with the high brimmed bonnets, mainly in summer to protect fair complexions. They were usually of black or white lace and when not worn over the bonnet were pushed back and worn for decoration, hanging down the shoulders from the brim.

Straw hats were still popular from the previous century, but were worn with smaller brims and round or flat crowns. They were held in place with ribbons tied under the chin, but placed over the hat, thus bending the brim down to give the appearance of a bonnet shape. Other styles; made also of chip, beaver, silks etc., could be similar but without a brim at the back so that the front poked out like an enormous peak. Turban or beret-type hats were also fashionable.

Round lace cap with lappets lace edged and tied under the chin. c. 1818

Silk poke bonnet with lace veil in front. c. 1806

Bonnet with feather plume c. 1800

LEFT: *The lady is wearing a large checked or plaid dress with a low decolletage and pointed bodice, c.1840.*
CENTRE: *The gathered fichu leaves a low decolletage, and the pointed bodice is fitted to a gathered skirt which is full, c.1840.*
RIGHT: *An evening dress worn as an open gown, the bodice close fitting to the waist with a low decolletage. The sleeves were of the beret type. Hair decoration was a mass of flowers, c.1830.*

LEFT: *Child's dress similar to an adult's, with sloping shoulders and full 'imbecile' sleeves. The apron was an added decoration. Drawers showed beneath the bottom of the dress, c.1831.*

CENTRE: *Gentleman in morning coat with pantaloons strapped under the shoes. He is wearing a top hat, c.1829.*

RIGHT: *The lady is wearing a dress in a popular striped material with gigot sleeves ending in tight fitting cuffs. The skirt is very full and gathered at the waist. The bonnet is wide brimmed with a deep bavolet at the back, c.1831.*

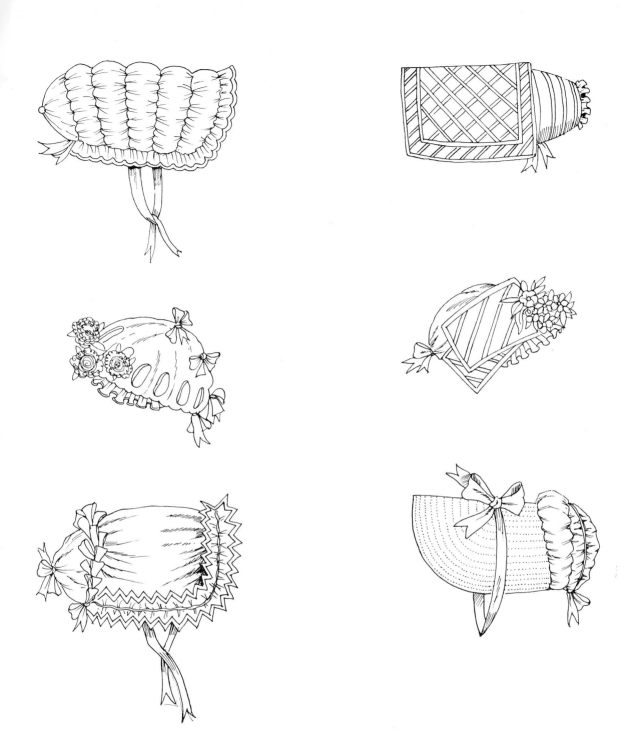

Hat styles of the first decade of the nineteenth century

Round or oval hats were the most common at the beginning of the century, as they were an ideal complement to short and classical hairstyles. Hats were mainly made of straw whilst for formal occasions satin was popular. Many hats were tied under the chin with either ribbon or a scarf, and were known under a great variety of names such as the 'Gypsy' hat which had a moderately wide brim, the 'village' hat with a brim turned up acutely front and back as well as other names.

Pamela type bonnet. c. 1815

About 1820 a type of bonnet with a dip in front of the brim was fashionable, but the ribbons which were tied under the chin were often allowed to hang down so that the sides of the brims were not pulled in. At this stage bonnets evolved into hats which then became larger and more lavishly decorated with an abundance of ribbon loops, flowers and leaves as well as ostrich feathers for evening wear. Some even had ornamentation either side of the brims. Leghorn and Dunstable straw were two of the popular materials used besides others such as velvet, and in 1826 washable cotton as well as transparent materials became popular.

Hats were often worn tilted towards the back of the head, so as not to disturb the curls, and had a downward curve from right to left. By the end of the 1820s, they were worn far back on the head with the brim in front tilted. When ribbons were added to the edge of the brim, hats again began to resemble bonnets.

Riding hats, mainly of black beaver were usually high crowned or had round crowns with shallow or tricorne brims. They were often decorated with hat bands and feathering.

HAIRSTYLES

Just before the beginning of the nineteenth century high headdresses had become unfashionable and had been replaced by long flowing curls and ringlets. Wide ribbon bands worn around the head were extremely popular and could be decorated with tall ostrich plumes, especially for formal and Court wear. The popularity of false hair and wigs went into decline, but padded rolls were still used for the fuller styles. Wigs, however could be worn with shorter hair styles. Hair powders were used less due to the tax imposed on them.

Most new hairstyles came from France, such as the 'Titus' or 'à la victime' cut — a style where the hair was cut short all over. Other variations allowed for the back to be left

Ladies hairstyles made up of false pieces with an ivory or tortoiseshell comb

Coiffure styles adorned with ribbons, flowers and small bonnets

long, hanging in ringlets. Short, close-curled hair was also favoured. Another popular fashion in the early part of the century was a Grecian style where the hair was pulled back and tied in curls or ringlets at the back. False hair was sometimes added to emphasise the Grecian look.

Roman and Oriental fashions were also popular with various names such as 'à la Egyptienne'. This was a style with the hair brushed back and caught with a comb highly decorated with precious stones, the hair being either plaited or coiled. The front hair was allowed to remain in soft waves with rows of beads across the forehead to the back. Hair in the Roman style was pulled back, ending in ringlets, with the front hair in curls, and a bandeau worn around the head.

After about 1814 the 'Titus' style was replaced by long hair. The classical styles gradually evolved into softer shapes with small ornate curls at the forehead and sides. Back hair could be plaited into a large top knot which, by the middle of the 1820s, became so complicated that it was arranged with loops and bows and held up with wire frames and glauvina pins. The more elaborate the coiffure became, the more ornamentation was required, such as jewellery, feathers, ribbons and flowers. 'Apollo' knots, for example, were pieces of hair, often false, emerging from a chignon. The hair still had a centre parting, around the forehead and the sides were in tight curls. The back hair was fastened in a chignon, but for evening wear ringlets would fall loosely down.

There were many variations of these styles with diverse names. Tall decorated combs were also used to give the required effect, these could be made of tortoiseshell or precious metals with inlaid jewels.

About 1829 hair 'à la Chinoise' was fashionable. The back and side hair was brushed straight up into a plaited chignon with close curls at the temples and forehead.

By about 1835 hairstyles again became lower with tall loops of hair or braided knots set at the back of the head. Hair partings could be centre or side, or either side with the hair in between brushed back, a cluster of curls falling either side. A centre parting with the hair dressed in various styles over the ears, either hanging ringlets or plaits looped up to a chignon at the back were just two of the many other variations. The back hair was often twisted into a knot with the spiral sides around the ears and caught at the back.

Ladies hair-style built up over a frame and decorated with flowers, c. 1830

52

Crocheted purse with tassels, used by both men and women. Also sometimes called a stocking purse. c. 1842

For evening wear the hair could be worn smooth in front and on top with the sides fluffed out into soft curls or a cluster of ringlets. False hair could be used to help pad out the fullness.

Another style for evening could have the side hair arranged in ringlets with a double parting converging at the front, the hair being combed back smoothly into a tall Apollo knot.

A ferronière — a narrow jewelled or gold chain — was worn around the head and over the forehead for either day or evening wear.

MAKE-UP

From the start of the nineteenth century rouge on the cheeks was very fashionable and cork or wax 'plumpers' (stuffing worn inside the mouth) to fill out the cheeks were still worn by a few. This fashion having been the mode in the previous century. Rouge became less popular from the late 1830s when it became fashionable to be pale and languid looking.

Aprons were a popular accessory usually embroidered and made of white muslin. They could have small pockets. For evening wear they were often made of white lace and could be frilled. From about 1836 they often had a bib and were wider with a ruched edge. They were popularly worn with morning or home dresses.

Handkerchiefs, mainly of cambric or cotton, could be lace edged for evening wear when carried in the hand. For mourning they were made of a black silk. *Handbags*, known as 'reticules' were diamond or round shaped and were carried to hold fans, purses and scent containers. They could also be suspended from the waist, often in the same colour as the dress itself. They were made of silks, satins or for evening wear in velvet with a drawstring or ribbon closure. In the 1820s a clasp of either steel or tortoise-shell became popular.

Gloves were above elbow length, of leather, silk or net. If made of a very soft leather they were worn in the evenings either long or short. By the 1830s gloves worn in daytime were short and mainly made of leather and embroidered on the backs. Evening gloves, until about 1836 could be long, after which date they became much shorter. They were often of white kid and could be embroidered and trimmed with ruching.

Short *mittens* were worn in the daytime whilst for evening wear they were worn long. *Muffs,* large about 1800, were made to match the boas and tippets in either fur or swan's down. They could also be of feathers. Muffs gradually became much smaller towards the 1840s.

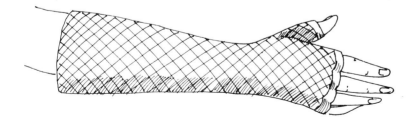

Long gauntlet type mittens.
c. 1835

Fans were fairly large at the start of the nineteenth century, smaller as the years went by, and were often decorated with painted scenes or pictures. In the 1830s the handles were often made of ornamented ivory or mother-of-pearl. For special occasions the fans could be of feather with elegant handles. Fan parasols were so made that the frame became a type of mask for the face, and although popular at the beginning of the century, they became much more fashionable in the 1840s.

Parasols were a popular accessory in the shape of a pagoda. The silk cover continued on the frame towards the ferule so that when opened the required shape was attained. The awnings were often fringed or edged with a lace border. Some parasols had the steel sticks made to telescope, and handles were often made of ivory or of gold and very decorative.

A great deal of *jewellery* was worn in the form of brooches, bracelets, necklaces and earrings as well as rings. Pendants were also popular as well as watches attached to dresses at the bosom. By about 1810 pendant earrings had made their mark. Watches were worn on a chain around the waist. Several gold chains were worn around the neck with scent cases, lockets or crosses suspended from them. Shell and cameo brooches as well as Eastern-influenced designs were worn in the 1820s.

In the 1830s short necklaces were very popular whilst long pendant earrings were often made in the shape of fruit or flowers, and bouquets of artificial flowers were also carried in the daytime as well as in the evenings. Brooches were also oblong and could be of mosaic or cameo.

Eyeglasses suspended from chains were worn throughout the period. Bracelets could also be worn as ring guards with a chain from the ring to the bracelet.

A 'jeanette' was a necklace made of tresses of hair or velvet ribbon from which a cross or heart could be suspended and was fashionable in the mid-1830s.

Girl in knee-length dress with
Marie sleeves, fichu and ankle-
length frilled pantaloons, c 1810

Boy in a waisted full-skirted
coat with full shoulder sleeves
which taper to fit tightly at
the wrist. Long pantaloons and
a top hat were worn, c. 1832

Very young boy in an ankle-
length frock with long frilled
at the bottom pantaloons. A
straw top hat was very popular,
c 1816

Children

Small boy in a belted smock frock with dagged collar and front edges. Ankle-length pantaloons and a mortar-board style hat, c. 1830

BOYS

Until the age of about five, boys wore similar fashions to little girls. After that age they wore trousers. In their teens they began to wear frock coats and flowered waistcoats and cravats, as well as either knee breeches or long trousers.

Until the 1830s young boys could wear a type of suit known as a 'skeleton suit'. This was a tight jacket with a double row of buttons fastening the front. Ankle-length trousers were buttoned to the jacket at the waistline. Long trousers could also be buttoned to the blouse or high up on the shirt, with a small jacket worn open to reveal the shirt frills.

Eton suits were worn by schoolboys throughout the century. The short jacket was single-breasted with square fronts, while the back was slightly pointed. The collar was of the turned-down type with wide lapels. The jacket was so cut that it was left open to reveal a waistcoat buttoned to the top, but leaving the bottom button undone. The jacket was originally in blue or red, but after 1820, with the death of George III, black was worn for mourning and the jacket has remained in this colour to this day. Knee breeches or pantaloons were also worn before that date; and trousers, mainly in grey, usually with the bottoms turned up, became the mode after 1820. The most characteristic appearance of the Eton suit was, apart from the short jacket, the white, starched 'Eton collar', which was rather wide with rounded corners and turned over the coat collar. It was worn with a white shirt and black tie.

Around 1810 little boys wore suits that resembled overalls, either long or short sleeved. Older boys wore their suits with a slight military flavour, due to the influence of the Napoleonic Wars. These suits could be decorated with braid and frogging on both the jacket and trousers. Shirts were fashionable with high necks and frilled collars.

A favourite outfit in the 1820s was a tight-fitting double-breasted short coat with a small velvet stand-up collar and a row of decorative buttons starting high on either side. Beneath this was worn a white blouse with a frilled and ruffled collar. To complete the outfit long ankle-length trousers were worn.

Caps, either peaked (with a tassel from the 1830s) or quartered, were worn as well as top hats and 'chimney-pot' hats. Boys' hair was short cut, becoming curly in the 1830s.

Boy in skeleton suit and a peaked quartered cap. c. 1820

Young girl in high waisted frock and pantelettes. c. 1810

High waisted lace frock with matching pantelettes. c. 1816

The gentleman with the two children is wearing breeches and stockings.
The young boy is in close fitting trousers. The girl is wearing a high
waisted style dress with a three quarter length cloak. c. 1799

Girls mainly dressed in a similar manner to their elders. At the start of the century the skirts were long and the necklines low. The dresses were usually short sleeved. Until the 1830s white drawers were worn which were ankle length with trousers as an alternative. These showed beneath the skirts. White cotton stockings were also worn whilst socks were only worn by the very small girls.

Headwear was always worn out of doors although indoor caps were not so popular. Although they had no school uniform as such, schoolgirls usually wore clothes similar to each other to give the appearance of uniformity and yet still remain fashionable. At the start of the century cotton materials had dainty designs, such as spots and sprigs woven into the material. Cottons as well as transparent materials were used for these dresses which were worn over coloured or white petticoats — a style profusely illustrated by Kate Greenaway. Sashes and fichues were very popular as were mob caps up to about 1805.

Before 1800 dresses were not too tight fitting with frilled collars and sleeve edges, but after that date the Empire line became fashionable and girls dresses had a yoke with the skirt gathered just under the arms. Dress collars were frilled and goffered, resembling small neck ruffs, whilst sleeves, either long or short, could be puffed with frilling at the wrists or the end of the puffs.

By about 1825 the Empire style became outdated, with the waistline falling back to normal; children's skirts became fuller as well as shorter with a belt or sash worn around the waist.

Pantaloons down to the ankles and in a matching design to the dress were very fashionable. The general shape of girls dresses, however, was much the same as the adults with the wide collars and sleeves, as well as the enormous and cumbersome hats.

Although small children rarely wore shoes or slippers, when they did the footwear was usually of kid or a soft leather in the matching colour to the clothes.

A small girl with a just below knee-length frock over which was worn a frilled-edged full apron. Large-brimmed bonnet with a bavolet was worn, c. 1833

*Little girl in a full skirted
dress with the waist at normal
level and pantelettes showing
beneath. c. 1830*

*Young lady in a full skirted
dress with pantelettes. c. 1835*

The 1827 style of ladies dresses. Right, a young lady in a large bonnet with the full sleeve at the elbow and tapering to a close-fitting frill at the wrist. Lady on the right has the popular bonnet and bavolet and the lace-edged shoulder cape (or fichu). The elbow sleeve has a double puff and then fits tightly at the wrist, c. 1827

Glossary

Aigret	Tuft of feathers.
Apollo Knot	Piece of false hair plaited or looped and wired to stand upright.
Babet	Small tulle bonnet worn in the evening, covering the back of the head over the ears.
Bag Wig	Powdered wig, the back tied into a black silk bag.
Banjan	Loose jacket worn informally in the mornings.
Basque	Short skirt added to bodice from the waist down.
Bavolet	Soft frill attached to back of bonnet, like a curtain at the back.
Beret Sleeve	Short wide sleeve cut circularly and gathered on to a band at the arm, resembling a beret.
Biggin	Form of mob cap without lappets.
Bishop Sleeve	Full sleeve from shoulder to wrist where it was gathered to a band.
Bodice	Upper part of a dress, a development from the word body. It is distinct from a blouse, as it is close fitting, a blouse being a separate article of clothing, and not joined to a skirt.
Bodice en Coeur	Heart shaped bodice front with narrow pleats at upper edge of the neckline.
Bodice à l'enfant	Rounded neckline gathered by a drawstring.
Bonnet	Head covering without a brim at the back, usually tied with a ribbon under the chin.
Bottines	Knee high riding boots.
Box Coat	Caped overcoat, at first mainly worn by coachmen.
Braces	Bands of material worn to hold up breeches or trousers.
Brandenburg Fastenings	Braided loops and buttons.

Breeches	Leg covering, like trousers but usually ending above the knees.
Brodequin	Velvet or satin boots with a fringe around the top.
Burnoise Mantle	Long evening wrap fastening at the neck, a hood could be attached.
Buskins	Knee high boots.
Bustle	Whalebone cage worn under a skirt to support the fullness at the back.
Button Stand	Separate pieces of material with buttons and buttonholes, sewn to the front of a garment in order to protect the cloth.
Calash	Folding hood on hoops.
Capote	Soft crowned bonnet with a stiffened brim.
Caul	Soft top of a bonnet or cap.
Chapeau Bras	Tricorne hat, usually flat and carried under the arm.
Chemise	Long, loose full garment.
Chemisette	White fill-in to a bodice, often with fine pleating down the centre front.
Clocks	Decoration on the outside edge of stockings or socks.
Clogs	Wooden soled overshoes.
Cornet	White day cap, tied under the chin.
Corset	Undergarment stiffened with whalebone or steel stays to support the bosom and make the waistline smaller by lacing.
Cottage Bonnet	Close-fitting straw bonnet with projecting brim.
Cravat	Necktie.
Crinoline	Petticoat usually stiffened with horsehair and worn with hoops.
Décolletage	Low neckline.
Deshabille	Undress.
Double-breasted	Overlapping fronts with a double row of buttons, one set used for fastening the jacket or coat.
Elastic Round Hat	Collapsible hat with a spring inside the crown.
Fall	Buttoned front fastening of breeches.
Ferronière	Narrow gold or jewelled band worn around the head with a jewel resting on the forehead.
Fichu	Softly draped collar.
Fichu-pelerine	Shoulder covering, sometimes with a double cape and turned-down collar, the fichu ends being down to knee level.
Fish Dart	Narrow dart shaped piece of material cut out of garment which is then sewn together to give a better shape without the bulkiness.
Flounce	Gathered or pleated frill used as ornamentation.
Fly	Strip of material to conceal the buttons and buttonhole fastening at the front of trousers.
Frock Coat	Tail coat with turned-down collar, becoming waisted and

	close-fitting from about 1816, buttoned to the waist with a back vent and side pleats with hip buttons.
Frogging	Looped braid fastening.
Gaiters	Ankle covering, spreading over the tops of shoes or boots, fastened with a strap under the instep, and generally buttoned on the outside.
Garters	Strip of material fastened around the legs to hold up stockings.
Gibus	Top hat with a collapsible crown, replaced the Elastic hat.
Gigot Sleeves	Full at the shoulder, becoming tight to the wrist, the top part could be distended by hoops.
Gores	Wedge shaped panels of material sewn together to give a flared appearance.
Habit Shirt	Fill-in for a day dress with sometimes a small neck ruff added.
Hessians	Calf length riding boots coming to a point in front at the top and decorated with a tassel, usually the boots were in black edged with a coloured leather border.
Highlows	Boots reaching the ankles and fastened in the front.
Imbecile Sleeve	Full sleeve gathered to a cuff at the wrist.
Jeanette	Necklace made of hair or velvet ribbon with a cross or heart suspended.
Kerseymere	Woollen cloth.
Lapel	Turned back upper part of front of a jacket or coat.
Mancherons	Short oversleeves worn on day dresses and outdoor garments, similar to epaulettes.
Mentonnières	Lace or tulle quillings added to the bonnet strings forming a frill under the chin, when tied.
Mittens	Short or long gloves leaving the fingers and thumb tips bare.
Mob Cap	Indoor cap with a frilled border.
Morning Coat	Riding coat also known as a Newmarket, the fronts sloping away from the waist with a back vent and two hip buttons.
Morning Gown	Long, loose coat with a sash or girdle around the waist, worn informally.
Moschettos	Similar to pantaloons, worn over boots like gaiters.
Muffs	Wide band of fur or thick material to keep the hands warm.
Muffetees	Small wrist muffs to keep the wrist warm.
Opera Hat	Soft crowned hat which could fold between the side brims — forerunner of the gibus.
Pantaloons	Close fitting shaped tights with short side slits worn by men. Ladies wore them as straight long legged drawers.
Parasol	Light ornamental umbrella used as protection against the sun.
Pattens	Platform soles to keep shoes off the ground.
Pelerine	Shoulder cape.
Pelisse	Three quarter length cape or cloak.

Pelisse Robe	Day dress fastened down the front with ribbon bows or hidden hooks and eyes.
Petersham Frock	Double-breasted with velvet collar, lapels and cuffs with flapped pockets.
Petticoat	Underskirt, of which several could be worn, the undermost usually being of flannel.
Pilot Coat	Double-breasted wide lapelled short overcoat with, usually a velvet collar.
Placket	Short opening or slit from the waistline down to facilitate passing the skirt over the head.
Pumps	Shoes with thin soles and low sided, could be decorated with a ribbon bow and worn for formal occasions.
Queue	Hanging tail of a wig.
Quizzing Glass	Monocle hanging from a chain around the neck.
Redingote	Close fitting gown fastening down the front, could be worn as a light overcoat.
Reticule	Small handbag.
Riding Habit	Costume designed for riding, usually consisting of a jacket and skirt decorated with braid and brandenburgs.
Robe	Type of gown or dress with an overdress, open in front, and long behind.
Robe à l'anglaise	Sack-back gown with sewn down pleats to waist level.
Roll Collar	See shawl collar.
Round Gown	Bodice and skirt in one, closed all round and without a train.
Ruff	Neck or wrist frill.
Sack Back	Pleats sewn from neckline to waist, then hanging down freely at the back.
Shawl	Wrap to cover the shoulders.
Shawl Collar	Broad turnover collar continuous with the lapels — later known as a roll collar.
Spatterdashes	Leggings reaching over the knees, fastened on the outside, they could also extend over the feet and be strapped beneath.
Spencer	Short waist length jacket for men with a rolled collar and cuffed sleeves. For ladies, short waist level jacket which could be sleeveless.
Spencerette	Tight fitting spencer with low cut neckline decorated with a lace frill.
Stock	High stiffened neck cloth.
Stomacher	Front part of a bodice.
Single-breasted	Single row of buttons fastening the front of a jacket or coat which does not overlap in the front.
Surtout	Overcoat made similar to a frock coat.
Tack-over	Overlap of a pleat at the top of a vent.

Taglioni Frock	Single breasted with short full skirts, broad collar and large cape, hip pockets and a back vent and tackover.
Tippet	Short shoulder cape.
Top Boots	Previously called jockey boots, reaching to just beneath the knees with the top of a lighter colour and turned over. Loops were used to aid the pulling on of these boots.
Topper or Top Hat	Tall high crowned hat with a narrow brim, sometimes rolled at the sides. From the 1830s also worn by women for riding.
Toque	Turban-like hat.
Tucker	Frilled edging in a soft material worn as a fill-in to a low decolletage.
Tunic Dress	Dress with an overskirt.
Turban	Headdress of material folded around the head.
Vent	Short slit from the hem of a garment upwards.
Wellington Frock	Single-breasted coat with a roll collar, but without lapels, buttoning to the waist, full skirted with back vent and side pleats. A horizontal dart at waist level.
Zona	Type of brassière.

Select Bibliography

Arnold, J., *Handbook of Costume*, Macmillan 1973

Arnold, J., *Patterns of Fashion* 2 Vols., Macmillan 1972

Asser, Joyce, *Historic Hairdressing*, Pitman 1966

Boehn, M. von, *Modes and Manners* (8 vols), Harrap 1926-35

Barfoot, A., *Everyday Costume in England*, Batsford 1966

Boucher, F., *History of Costume in the West*, Thames & Hudson 1967;
  20,000 Years of Fashion, Abrams

Bradfield, N., *Costume in Detail, Women's Dress 1730-1930* Harrap;
  Historical Costumes of England, Harrap 1958

Brooke, Iris, *History of English Costume*, Methuen 1937;
  English Children's Costume, A & C. Black 1965;
  Western European Costume, Theatre Arts Books 1963

Buck, Anne, *Victorian Costume & Costume Accessories*, Herbert Jenkins 1961

Calthrop, D.C., *English Costume*, A & C. Black 1906 — Book Five only

Cassin-Scott, J., *Costume & Fashion 1760-1920* Blandford 1971

Contini, M., *The Fashion from Ancient Egypt to the Present Day*, Hamlyn 1967

Cooke, P.C., *English Costume*, Gallery Press 1968

Courtais, G. de, *Women's Headdress and Hairstyles*, Batsford 1971

Cunnington, C.W., P.E., *Costume in Pictures*, Studio Vista; *Handbook of English
  Costume in the 19th Century* Faber & Faber 1954; *Dictionary of Costume 900-1900*,
  A & C. Black 1970

Cunnington & Buck, *Childrens Costume in England 1300-1900*, A & C. Black 1965

Davenport, M., *The Book of Costume*, Bonanza 1968

De Antfrasio, Charles & Roger, *History of Hair*, Bonanza 1970

Dorner, Jane, *Fashion*, Octopus 1974

Fairholt, F.W., *Costume in England*, 1885

Francoise, Lejeune, *Histoite due Costume*, Editions Delalain

Garland, M., *The Changing Face of Beauty*, Weidenfield & Nicolson 1957;
  History of Fashion, Orbis 1975

Gibbs-Smith, Charles, *The Fashionable Lady in the 19th Century*, H.M.S.O. 1960

Gorsline, D., *What people wore*, Bonanza

Hansen, H., *Costume Cavalcade*, Methuen 1956

Harrison, Molly, *Hairstyles and Hairdressing*, Ward Lock 1968

Hartnell, N., *Royal Courts of Fashion*, Cassell 1971

Holland, V., *Hand Coloured Fashion Plates 1770-1899*, Batsford 1955

Kelly, Mary, *On English Costume*, Deane 1934

Koehler, C., *History of Costume*, Constable 1963

Laver, James, *Concise History of Costume*, Thames & Hudson 1963; *Costume*, Batsford 1956; *Costume Through the Ages*, Thames & Hudson 1964

Lister, Margot, *Costume*, Herbert Jenkins 1967

Moore, D., *Fashion Through Fashion Plates 1771-1970*, Ward Lock 1971

Norris, Herbert, *Costume and Fashion*, J.M. Dent 1924

Pistolese & Horstig, *History of Fashions*, Wiley 1970

Rupert, J., *Le Costume*, Flammarion 1930

Saint-Laurent, C., *History of Ladies Underwear*, Michael Joseph 1968

Truman, N., *Historic Costuming*, Pitman 1936

Waugh, Norah, *The cut of Mens Clothes 1600-1900* Faber & Faber 1964
The cut of Womens Clothes 1600-1930 Faber & Faber 1968

Wilcox, R.T., *Dictionary of Costume*, Batsford 1970; *The Mode in Costume*, Scribner's 1942; *The Mode in Hats and Headdress*, Scribner's 1948

Wilson, E., *History of Shoe Fashions*, Pitman 1969

Yarwood, D., *English Costume from the 2nd Century BC to the Present Day*, Batsford 1975; *Outline of English Costume*, Batsford 1967

Pictorial Encyclopedia of Fashion, Hamlyn 1968

Index